Go, Critter, Go!
Squirm, Earthworm, Squirm!

Dana Meachen Rau

Marshall Cavendish
Benchmark
New York

Earthworms are pink.

Earthworms are
smooth.

Earthworms can be long.

Earthworms can be short.

Earthworms eat
through dirt.

11

Earthworms dig
tunnels.

Earthworms are food for birds.

Earthworms like rain.

17

Squirm, earthworm, squirm!

Words We Know

bird

dirt

long

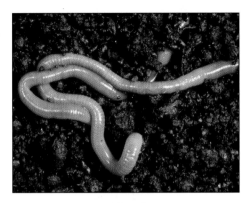

pink

short

smooth

tunnel

Index

Page numbers in **boldface** are illustrations.

About the Author

Dana Meachen Rau is an author, editor, and illustrator. A graduate of Trinity College in Hartford, Connecticut, she has written more than one hundred fifty books for children, including nonfiction, biographies, early readers, and historical fiction. She lives with her family in Burlington, Connecticut.

With thanks to the Reading Consultants:

Nanci Vargus, Ed.D., is an Assistant Professor of Elementary Education at the University of Indianapolis.

Beth Walker Gambro received her M.S. Ed. Reading from the University of St. Francis, Joliet, Illinois.

Marshall Cavendish Benchmark
99 White Plains Road
Tarrytown, New York 10591-9001
www.marshallcavendish.us

Library of Congress Cataloging-in-Publication Data

Rau, Dana Meachen, 1971–
Squirm, earthworm, squirm! / by Dana Meachen Rau.
p. cm. — (Bookworms. Go, critter, go!)
Summary: "Describes characteristics and behaviors of earthworms"—Provided by publisher.
Includes index.
ISBN-13: 978-0-7614-2650-9
1. Earthworms—Juvenile literature. I. Title. II. Series.
QL391.A6R38 2007
592'.64—dc22
2006034230

Editor: Christina Gardeski
Publisher: Michelle Bisson
Designer: Virginia Pope
Art Director: Anahid Hamparian

Photo Research by Anne Burns Images

Cover Photo by *Photo Researchers*/E.R. Degginger

The photographs in this book are used with permission and through the courtesy of:
Animals Animals: pp. 1, 19 Breck P. Kent; pp. 3, 21TL Color-Pic; pp. 9, 17, 21TR Donald Specker;
pp. 13, 21BR David M. Dennis; pp. 15, 20TL Patti Murray. *Peter Arnold Inc.*: pp. 5, 21BL Ed Reschke.
Corbis: pp. 7, 20B Eric & David Hosking. *Photo Researchers*: pp. 11, 20TR Dr. Jeremy Burgess.

Printed in Malaysia
1   3   5   6   4   2